MW01678664

in the

Old Roxy

A Lemon Street Gang Adventure

MARY BLAKESLEE

MOONSTONE PRESS

Cover Art by Sheri Helferty.
Designed and produced by MonaChrome Design, Port Elgin, Ontario
Printed and bound in Canada by Kromar Printing Ltd., Winnipeg.

Moonstone Press gratefully acknowledges the financial assistance of The Canada Council and the Ontario Arts Council.

Canadian Cataloguing in Publication Data

Blakeslee, Mary
The ghost in the old Roxy

"A Lemon Street gang adventure".
ISBN 0-920259-48-0

I. Title.

PS8553.L3G5 1993 jC13'.54 C93-094643-X
BZ7.B53Gh 1993

Moonstone Press
175 Brock Street
Goderich, Ontario
Canada N7A 1R4

For Caroline Dunsmore with love

Chapter One

"WHAT'S that creepy building up there on the hill standing all by itself?" Penny Campbell asked. "It looks like something out of a Stephen King novel."

"That's the old Roxy Theatre," David Shaw answered. "It hasn't been used for years now, but my Dad said when he was a little kid back in the fifties it still ran movies."

"Yeah," Jason Ogilvie chimed in, "they closed it down when TV came to Pinterville, and everyone stopped going to the show. They say it's haunted."

"Oh, come on, Jase," David chided. "That's just a story somebody got going to scare kids from wrecking the place."

"I'm not so sure. Matthew told me his cousin told him her boyfriend saw it with his own eyes."

"Boy, that's real reliable evidence, isn't it?" Gerry Reece laughed.

"Gee, it sounds exciting," Penny exclaimed. "Could we go take a look?"

"I don't think that's such a hot idea," Jason muttered at the same time as David was saying, "Sure, why not?"

Penny and Gerry gave Jason a puzzled look. He blushed and stammered, "It's not that I'm scared or anything, but the place isn't safe. The wood's decaying and the foundation's cracking and . . ."

"Okay, we get it," David nodded. "We'll be careful. Actually, I've always wondered about the old place myself. It should be fun to explore it. But, it's almost five and I told Mrs. Jarvis we'd be home by five-thirty for dinner. How about we check it out later this evening."

All three looked inquiringly at Jason. "Sure," he agreed with a show of bravado. As the recognized leader of the Lemon Street Gang there was no way Jason Ogilvie, age eleven, was going to let his friends see how uncomfortable he was with the idea of actually going into that place. And at night, at that.

David, Gerry and Penny left Jason at his house and walked up the block to David's where the two visitors from the city were staying.

Unlike Gerry, Penny was not an official member of the Lemon Street Gang. David and Jason had met her earlier that summer when they were visiting Gerry, who had moved from Pinterville to the city the previous year. Because of her extreme bravery during an incident at the East End Mall the boys had invited her to become an honourary member of the gang. So when Gerry came back to Pinterville for his annual visit, Penny was invited to come with him.

David and Jason had spent the first day of their visitors' week long stay showing Penny the sights. Gerry was, of course, familiar with the small town and not terribly thrilled with the tour, but Penny, having lived in the big city all her life, was enchanted by everything she saw.

"Too bad you guys couldn't have come a few days earlier," Jason had remarked when they passed the fair grounds. "Pioneer Days ended last Sunday. Those fair grounds were crowded with people in vans and campers and tents until yesterday. Now all that's left is that weird looking van with the pictures of wild animals on it."

"Do they still have the big lottery?" Gerry asked.

"Yeah, but this year was a disaster. Somebody got off with all the money — about three hundred thousand dollars, I heard."

"That's right," David agreed. "Dad's on the committee that organizes the lottery. Apparently the money was put into the safe at the Chamber of Commerce building on Sunday night when Pioneer Days ended. They drew the lucky number at midnight and the winner was given a cheque for two hundred thousand dollars. They were supposed to take the cash to the bank Monday morning so the cheque would clear. But when they opened the safe it was empty."

"Do they have any idea who took the money?" Gerry asked.

"There were only two people who knew the combination of the safe," David replied. "Colonel Blunt, the chairman of the Pioneer Days committee, and Ronnie Albright, the manager of the Chamber of Commerce. Ronnie hasn't been seen or heard from since Sunday night."

"Ronnie Albright," Gerry mused. "Isn't he that kid who got sent away to a juvenile detention centre for robbing a 7 Eleven about five years ago?"

"That's him," Jason nodded. "He came back to Pinterville about six months ago, and Colonel Blunt talked the city into hiring him to run the Chamber. Everyone agreed he'd paid his debt to society and should be given another chance. He was doing really well, too. Until last Sunday, that is."

"I just can't believe he took the money." David shook his head. "He was trying so hard to make it. My Dad said the Chamber had never been run so well."

"Yeah, I know," Jason agreed, "but if he didn't do it, why did he disappear?"

David didn't have an answer for that.

When they reached David's house they saw Mr. Shaw's car parked in the driveway.

"Oh, great!" David exclaimed. "Dad's home." He broke away and ran up the steps. "Hey, Dad," he yelled throwing open the front door. A moment later a distinguished-looking man in his fifties came out into the hallway. David rushed in, followed by the other two.

"Well, this must be the famous Penny Campbell I've heard so much about," Mr. Shaw greeted them. "And Gerry Reese. Good to see you again. We miss you around here."

"When did you get in, Dad?" David asked as they moved into the living room.

"A couple of hours ago. I flew into Calgary this morning and drove up this afternoon."

David's father was a very successful businessman with contacts all over the continent. Although it would have been easier for him to live in the city, when his wife had died leaving him to raise their six year old son alone he decided to return to the small town where he had grown up and where he felt it would be a safer and healthier place for David. Mrs. Jarvis, the housekeeper and surrogate mother to David, had been with them since the day they returned to Pinterville. She ruled the household, as Mr. Shaw liked to remark, with an iron hand in a velvet glove.

They had just nicely settled down when a very tall, very thin woman with iron-gray hair standing out from her head and making her look like dandelion gone to seed burst into the room.

"Ah, you're home," she told them unnecessarily. "Now upstairs with the lot of you and wash those hands. Dinner will be on the table in five minutes." She turned abruptly and hurried back to the kitchen.

"Mrs. Jarvis has spoken," David's father laughed. "If I were you I would obey."

The three children rose as one and hurried to the upstairs bathroom. In less than five minutes they were seated demurely at the dining room table with their hands in front of them for Mrs. Jarvis's inspection. Penny's eyes were as round as saucers, while Gerry and David, who were used to this drill, tried vainly to control their laughter.

"Well, I've seen cleaner, but I suppose it will do, bein's how this is somethin' of an occasion." She picked up a large casserole and passed it to Mr. Shaw. "Eat up now, you're lookin' peaked. All that flyin' around and eatin' goodness what — it does horrible things to the liver."

Mr. Shaw winked at the boys and meekly obeyed.

Chapter Two

"HAVE you heard anything more about the missing lottery money, Dad?" David asked as they were finishing dessert.

"Not a thing. It certainly looks bad for Ronnie Albright, I'm sorry to say. I really hoped he was serious about wanting to make a new start, but, well, the evidence . . ."

"Yeah, . . . points right to him," David finished. "Where do you think he went?"

"Probably took the late night bus to Calgary, then who knows after that. He could be anywhere in the world right now. The theft wasn't discovered until Monday morning, giving him a good twelve-hour head start."

"I don't believe it for a minute," Mrs. Jarvis asserted as she began collecting the dirty dishes. "That nice young man is no criminal."

"I'd like to think you were right, Mrs. Jarvis," David's father answered, "but look at the evidence: he disappeared and hasn't been seen since the robbery; he and Amos Blunt were the only ones who knew the combination to the safe; and he has a criminal record."

"Now don't be cloudin' the issue with facts, Mr. S. It only confuses things. I know what I know. Ronnie Albright always helped me with my groceries, and he even came over when you were away and helped me with the storm windows. No, it's as plain as the nose on your face. He's being framed." She picked up the last of the dishes and marched angrily back to the kitchen.

Mr. Shaw shook his head and laughed. "When Mrs. Jarvis gets an idea in her head, you couldn't get it out with a blow torch."

As they all rose from the table and started for the family room, David stopped and spoke to his father.

"Penny wants to check out the old Roxy Theatre, Dad. Is it okay if we go up there for awhile?"

"I don't know, David. The place is practically falling apart at the seams. It may not be safe."

"We'll be very careful, honest. We won't go any farther than the main floor. Nothing can happen to us."

"I suppose you're right. But be home before dark, and don't go fooling around in the balconies. They could be dangerous. And watch out for the ghost," he chuckled.

"Sure, Dad. And if we see Elvis we'll say hi to him for you."

Ten minutes later the three friends were on their way to pick up Jason.

"Too bad Matthew and Kyle aren't home," Jason remarked as they approached the old theatre. The other two members of the Lemon Street Gang were both on vacation with their parents and wouldn't be back in Pinterville until school started in two weeks.

"Yeah, Jase," David grinned. "We sure could use some extra man power against that ghost. As it is, we're only four against one."

"Can it, will you, Dave. If you think I'm scared you're nuts." And with that he broke away and ran up the hill to the decrepit building and threw open the door.

When the other three caught up with him he was standing in the far right aisle peering down into the theatre.

"Yuck, this place smells awful," Gerry remarked as they joined Jason at the head of the aisle. Although it was still light outside, the inside of the building was dim and gloomy. At first it was difficult to see anything, but as their eyes adjusted to the darkness they were able to see down into the pit of the theatre at what was left of the seats. Many had been removed and the ones that remained had been ravaged by animals and time.

"Mice and mildew mostly," David remarked. "Boy, it really is a mess, isn't it?"

"Look at those balconies," Penny pointed up to the small overhangings to the left and right.

"I think those are called boxes," David said. "That's where the rich people sat. The balconies are up above us."

Penny moved farther down the aisle and turning around, looked up.

Then she screamed.

"Penny, what's the matter?" Jason cried rushing

down toward her. A moment later Gerry and David joined them.

"There's something up there," Penny whispered in a trembling voice.

"Where?" the boys asked in unison.

"Up in that second balcony. See, over there on the right."

The boys looked up to where she was pointing. David gasped.

In the dim light what appeared to be a man dressed in old-fashioned formal attire was leaning over the rail.

"Oh my gosh! He looks like that guy in the old movie we saw last night. The one in the top hat who danced all the time."

"Fred Astaire," Gerry nodded. "He's dead, you know."

"Ohhh, then maybe it really is a ghost," Jason moaned.

At that moment the form turned and disappeared.

"Let's get out of here," Gerry muttered. "It's too creepy."

"That was no ghost," David insisted. "Someone was really up there."

"Well, I'm not sticking around to find out who it was," Jason said. "I never liked this place before, and I like it even less now."

"I'm with you, Jase," Gerry groaned. "Whether that thing is real or not, he can have the place."

Jason and Gerry turned and headed back up the aisle, Penny closely behind them. David stood alone for a minute or two longer gazing up at the balcony where the spectre had appeared. Then he, too, turned and joined the others.

"He was wearing a black coat, longer at the back, and black pants. He had on this big tall hat and his face was white," David finished.

"Oh, you kids," Mr. Shaw laughed. "You really did get taken in by that old story about a ghost haunting the theatre, didn't you?"

"It wasn't a ghost, Dad. It was real," David insisted.

"I'm sure you think it was real, son, but your imagination can play pretty nasty tricks on you. You said the theatre was unlit; it was likely just a shadow or a curtain moving. You expected to see a ghost — admit it, now — and so you did."

"It was awfully dark in the theatre, Dave," Gerry admitted.

"And what we thought we saw was a long way off."

"Yeah," Jason agreed, "I suppose it was just our imaginations."

David looked over at his three friends sitting at the kitchen table drinking pop while Mr. Shaw perched on the kitchen counter and listened to their wild tale. Jason and Gerry shrugged their shoulders and looked down at their glasses. Penny caught David's eye and shook her head. David smiled.

"I don't care what you think, Gerry, I believe there really was someone on that balcony. Penny thinks so, too."

"Well, Jason doesn't. That makes two against two."

David and Gerry were in David's room getting ready for bed and discussing the evening's events. Penny had left them a few minutes earlier to retire for the night in the Shaw's guest room.

"Jason isn't himself when he's anywhere around the fair grounds, Gerry," David said, trying to find a logical excuse for his friend's unusual behaviour. "He never really got over what happened to him last summer when the carnival was here. The fair grounds reminds him of what he went through and he gets strange."

"Well, I suppose you could be right. So what do we do about it? No one will believe us if we try to tell them. Look what happened with your father."

"I think we should go back for another look. Only this time we'll be a lot more careful. We won't go barging through the front door making enough noise to wake the dead and alert whoever is in there. We'll go in the back way, through the emergency exit door. I noticed it when we were standing in the aisle. It's partially open."

"And what do we do when we get in?"

"Look for whoever it is that's trying to scare us. It's probably some old tramp who's taken over the place for his home."

"A tramp that dresses like a dead movie star?"

"Well, yeah, you do have a point there," David admitted. "I don't know who it is or why he's hanging out in an abandoned theatre. That's what we're going to find out tomorrow night. I don't think I'd better tell Dad what we plan to do, though. He might forbid us from going. We'll wait until he and Mrs. Jarvis have gone to bed then we'll sneak out."

"Just the two of us or do we take Penny and Jason?"

"Take them, of course. Jase is really very smart and very brave, regardless of how he seems to be around that theatre. And Penny is braver than any of us."

"Okay, sounds good. But I'll bet we won't see anyone. I still think your Dad's right. We're all suffering from overactive imaginations."

"Maybe," David answered. "We'll find out tomorrow night, won't we?"

Chapter Three

DAVID and his two house guests were up shortly after eight the next morning. Mrs. Jarvis was doling out French toast and bacon when Mr. Shaw came downstairs and joined them at the kitchen table.

"Gee, Dad, you really slept in," David remarked as his father sat down across from him. "You're usually up with the birds."

"Colonel Blunt came by after you kids went to bed," his father explained. "As you know, I'm on the lottery committee for Pioneer Days. Amos Blunt wanted to confer with me about the missing money and what we should do about it."

"What's going to happen if they don't recover the money?" Penny asked.

"That's what we're trying to decide. Esther Cookson, the woman who won the lottery, is a single parent with three young children. The two hundred thousand would have made all the difference in the world to her. And, of course, the Historical Society really needed the hundred thousand that would have gone to it. There's no way the committee can come up with replacement funds, so it looks like Mrs.

Cookson and the Historical society will lose out."

"Unless they catch the thief," Gerry added.

"I'm afraid there's little chance of that. Ronnie Albright's probably hundreds of miles away by now. But the police have put out an all points bulletin for him, and his picture is being circulated by the R.C.M.P."

"Are the police sure Ronnie is the culprit?" Penny asked. "I mean, are they still investigating the possibility that it could be someone else?"

"Sergeant Collins was right on top of it as soon as the theft was discovered," Mr. Shaw answered. "She had the safe checked for fingerprints and found only Ronnie's and Colonel Blunt's. And, of course, they have been interviewing people and generally carrying out a thorough investigation. Maria Collins is a very thorough police officer."

"You said Ronnie probably took the bus on Sunday night,"David mused. "Did they find anyone at the bus depot who saw him?"

"Yeah, and what about the guy who sells tickets?" Gerry added.

"The bus depot was like a zoo Sunday night," David's father told them. "All the out-of-town visitors who had come up for Pioneer Days were on their way home. No one remembers seeing Ronnie in that crowd."

"So maybe Ronnie didn't take the money and run off," David said eagerly. "Maybe he just got scared when he heard the money was missing and hid out somewhere."

"My sentiments exactly," Mrs. Jarvis, who was listening to this exchange with a disbelieving look on her face, finally spoke. "The poor young lad. He's probably terrified, what with the whole town thinkin' he's a thief and out to get him." She slapped down a plate of French toast in front of Mr. Shaw and marched back to the kitchen.

"And just how would he know the money was missing?" David's father asked, ignoring Mrs. Jarvis's outburst. "When the theft was discovered Ronnie was nowhere around."

"Oh, yeah. I didn't think about that. I suppose he wouldn't disappear if he didn't have anything to hide."

"I'm afraid that's the case, Son. Amos Blunt is very upset about the whole thing, as you can imagine. It was on his recommendation that Ronnie was hired. He feels personally responsible for the loss of the money."

He picked up the morning paper beside his plate and began to read. A moment later Mrs. Jarvis returned with a coffee pot and, standing behind Mr. Shaw's chair, began filling his cup.

"Well, would you look at that?" she exclaimed, peering at the newspaper over Mr. Shaw's shoulder.

"What is it, Mrs. Jarvis?" David asked.

"It says here the Ideal Deli was broken into last night."

"Oh, gee," Jason exclaimed. "Poor Mr. Garibaldi. He's having a tough enough time trying to make it with that new deli chain opening up across the street. How much money was taken?"

"It don't say. Just that the thief got off with a considerable amount of merchandise."

"Maybe it was some poor kid who ran away from home and was living on the streets," Penny suggested.

"Not likely around here," Gerry answered. "Unless things have changed a lot since I moved away, Pinterville just doesn't have street people like in the big city."

"You're right, Gerry," Mr. Shaw agreed. "No, it was probably that bunch of rowdy kids that came up for Pioneer Days. They were camping out in that painted van at the fair grounds."

Just then the doorbell rang and a moment later Mrs. Jarvis ushered in a short fat roly-poly man with a fringe of gray hair circling his bald head.

"Ah, Amos," Mr. Shaw said, rising and beckoning the newcomer to a chair. "Sit down and join us. We're just finishing up our breakfast."

The man lowered his considerable bulk into a kitchen chair and beamed at the group across from him. "Ah, young David. Nice to see you again. And if I'm not mistaken, you're Gerald Reese."

"Right, and this is their friend, Penny Campbell. Penny, this is Colonel Blunt. Gerry and Penny are visiting here for a couple of weeks, Amos. Now, can I offer you anything?"

"Just coffee, thanks, Jonas."

Mrs. Jarvis brought a cup from the kitchen and proceeded to pour out the coffee. About half of it sloshed into the saucer.

"Sorry about that," Mrs. Jarvis mumbled with a frown and banged out of the room.

Colonel Blunt began pouring the coffee from the saucer into his cup while David's father handed him paper napkins, all the while apologizing in a voice loud enough to be heard in the kitchen.

The children exchanged glances and David whispered, “She doesn’t like him very much.”

“No joke?” Gerry laughed. “I never would have guessed it.”

When the coffee had been cleaned up Mr. Shaw said, “And what brings you here so early in the morning, Amos? Has there been a new development in the lottery theft?”

“There certainly has.” Colonel Blunt nodded his head vigorously and took a mouthful of coffee. “I got a call about an hour ago from Ronnie Albright. Said he wanted to thank me for recommending him for the job and to apologize to me for stealing the lottery money. Said the temptation was just too much. Sounded downright contrite, but that doesn’t get the money back.”

“Well, I’ll be . . .!” Mr. Shaw gasped. “The nerve of the young man. Any idea where he was calling from?”

“None. Only that it was long distance. He had to deposit a lot of change for the call. The operator had an American accent so I expect he’s somewhere across the border. No, Jonas, I’m afraid the money is gone for good. I reported the call to Sergeant Collins immediately, of course, and she called off any further investigation. Now we can only hope he’ll be recognized by the pictures the R.C.M.P. have circulated.”

They went on to discuss the possibilities open to them to solicit funds from private donors and local clubs in order to give at least a token payment to Esther Cookson. David motioned to Gerry and Penny and the three children got up from the table.

"What are your plans for today?" Mr. Shaw asked as they started to leave the room.

"I guess we'll pick up Jason and maybe take Penny to the mall so she can do some shopping," David answered. "We really don't know."

"Okay, but make sure you're back here for lunch. I thought we might drive up to the lake and go swimming this afternoon."

"Great! We'll see you around noon."

"Take Penny to the Mall! What's come over you, Dave?" Gerry exclaimed as they were walking down the street toward Jason's house. "You know you hate shopping."

"Yeah," Penny chimed in, "and after my experience last month if I never see another mall again it will be too soon."

"Cool it, guys," David answered. "It was just an excuse. We're not going to the mall; we're going to visit the Ideal Deli."

"Why?" David asked.

"To talk to Mr. Garibaldi, of course. How else are we going to get the clues we need to discover who broke into his store?"

Who's store?" Jason bounded out of his the house and joined the gang just in time to hear David's last remark.

"Mr. Garibaldi's," David answered. "Someone broke into the Ideal Deli and took a bunch of stuff."

"Your Dad said it was probably some kids that were

camping at the fair grounds," Gerry reminded him.

"Maybe, but I don't think so. Remember when we passed the fair grounds yesterday afternoon the only thing left was that painted van?"

"Yeah, sure."

"But last night it wasn't there!" Jason exclaimed, catching on to David's thinking. "So you figure the campers had left town before the robbery, Dave?"

"Yeah, and if they had, then someone else is responsible for the robbery."

"Got any ideas?" Penny asked.

"Maybe. Let's go talk to Mr. Garibaldi first. Okay?"

"Right on!" Jason cried. "I can see the headlines now: Another vicious crime solved by the illustrious Lemon Street Gang."

Chapter Four

A LOUD bell rang out over the door as the four kids entered the Ideal Deli a few minutes later. The place was empty. Then from behind a curtain at the back a tiny little man with thinning black hair and a luxurious black mustache hurried into the room.

"Ah, Davie, Davie. And Jasie, too. How nice of you to come see me." He rushed over and threw his arms around both boys. "You heard about my trouble?"

"Yes, that's why we're here. You remember Gerry Reece? And this is our friend from the city, Penny Campbell."

Mr. Garibaldi nodded and smiled while rubbing his hands together. "Come sit down here in the back. I'll get you a pop." He led the group to the room behind the curtain and went back to take four cans of soda from the cooler.

When everyone was settled, David began. "We want to help find who robbed you, Mr. Garibaldi. Do you mind if we ask you some questions?"

Mr. Garibaldi's eyes twinkled, but he answered solemnly, "No, no. Of course not. Ask away."

"Fine. Now when did you first discover that the

store had been robbed?"

"When I came back last night about eleven o'clock. I close up at nine and I'd gone home. Then I remembered I'd forgotten to put out an order for the dairy — Mac comes around about five in the morning — so I went back to leave him a note. That's when I saw the place had been broken into and stuff taken."

"People seem to think it was that gang of kids from the city, the ones in the wild painted van."

"No, no. Impossible." Mr. Garibaldi shook his head vehemently. "Those boys came into the store just after seven and bought a bunch of stuff. They were leaving for home and were planning to camp out again on the way back. I saw them drive off half an hour later."

"They could have circled back after you'd closed up and broken in," Jason suggested. "They probably saw you had money in the cash register."

"Sure I did. Quite a lot. But you don't understand. No money was taken. Just food."

"They didn't touch the till?" David asked eagerly. "Are you sure?"

"Of course, I'm sure, Davie. I left nearly fifty dollars in the till and not a penny of it was missing."

"Maybe I was right, then, about some hungry street kid taking the stuff," Penny said with a triumphant grin.

"No, I don't think so," David answered. Then turning back to Mr. Garibaldi he asked, "Is there anything else you can tell us?"

"Only that the thief was very tidy. I would hardly have known anything was taken if I hadn't gone to the dairy case to see what I needed to order and noticed a big hole where the mild cheddar cheese was supposed to be. Then I did some more checking and saw a lot of cold meat was missing. I didn't look any further; I called the cops. But I suspect there is a lot of packaged stuff missing — you know, crackers, cookies, bread."

"Any canned goods?" David asked.

"I don't think so. I did a quick check this morning, and there didn't seem to be any obvious gaps in the shelves. I'll know better when I do an inventory, but I think the thief only took stuff he could eat from the package; finger food."

"Thanks a lot, Mr. Garibaldi," David said as he stood up and put his empty pop can on the table beside him. "You've been very helpful."

"So, Davie, do you think you can solve the mystery for me?" Mr. Garibaldi's eyes twinkled again and a small smile played around his lips.

"Yes, sir. I think so," David answered solemnly.

"Okay, Dave, so what do you know that we don't?" Gerry demanded as they were walking back to the Shaw house.

"Nothing for sure. Just a hunch. Look, you guys, Gerry and I decided to go back to the old theatre tonight and see if we can get another look at the so-called ghost. Are you and Penny game to go with us?"

"Absolutely," Penny answered. "But will your Dad let us go out at night?"

"Probably not. That's why we're going to sneak out

after he and Mrs. Jarvis have packed it in for the night. What about you, Jase? Can you get away — and do you want to?" he added.

"Sure to both questions. I've snuck out my bedroom window so many times it practically opens itself. But I bet we won't run into any ghost. Like your Dad said, it was probably just our imagination."

"You hope," Penny laughed. "But I'm with David. I think there really is something there, and I don't believe it's any phantom."

David gave her a grateful smile. "I don't either."

They had reached Jason's house and stopped.

"Dad's taking us out to the lake to swim," he told Jason. "Do you want to come with us?"

"Sure, but I'll have to ask my Mom. What time are you going?"

"Right after lunch. We'll pick you up about one. And Jase, do you think the twins would let us borrow their water skis?"

"I don't know, but I can try. They come home for lunch, and since they're both working they won't need them this afternoon."

Since Mike and Johnny, Jason's eighteen-year-old brothers, had taught Jason and his friends to water ski the summer before, none of them could get enough of it.

As it turned out the twins were willing to lend their skis, and the gang spent a wonderful afternoon swimming and water skiing behind Mr. Shaw's power boat. For five hours no one thought of the break-in and the evening of sleuthing ahead of them.

However, when they returned just in time for an

early supper all the events of the morning were brought back to them. Mrs. Jarvis was full of the news and could barely contain herself.

"My lands!" she began as soon as the group entered the house. "You've missed all the excitement. They caught the fellow that robbed the Ideal Deli!"

"They did?" David stopped half way up the stairs and turned to give her a baffled look.

"Indeed they did. Caught him red-handed, sittin' behind the old court house eatin' a bag of cookies. Cookies," she added with the satisfied smile of one who knows justice has been done and evil punished, "with the Ideal Deli label on them."

"Who was it?" Mr. Shaw asked.

"Some old drunk. Should have been locked away long ago. My lands, I don't know what this town is comin' to," she said, repeating her favourite comment on the state of the community.

"Did he confess?" David asked, moving back down the stairs.

"No, of course not. Said he found them over by the fair grounds. A likely story!"

"I see." David smiled and caught Penny's eye. She winked back. Obviously, they were on the same wave length. The drunk the police had caught was not the 'ghost' that they had seen in the old Roxy. Now all they had to do was confirm their suspicions. And unless he was mistaken, David was pretty sure they would do that later on that night.

David, Penny and Gerry spent the evening playing

Monopoly to pass the time until Mr. Shaw and Mrs. Jarvis decided to retire for the night. The kids were allowed to stay up past their usual bedtime since it was still summer vacation. Mrs. Jarvis went to her room a little after nine but Mr. Shaw continued to sit in the living room reading a book.

Penny had hotels on both Park Place and Boardwalk and was threatening to bankrupt David when he landed on one and then on the other. Only half paying attention to the game he forked over the remainder of his money and stood up. He looked at his watch: ten after ten.

"Think I'll turn in," he announced in a loud voice, hoping his father would take the hint.

A moment later Mr. Shaw appeared at the door to the family room. "Guess I'll call it a day, too," he said, stretching and yawning. I'm going to have to get to the office early in the morning."

Penny and Gerry immediately took the hint. "Guess we'll hit the hay, too," Gerry announced in a hearty voice that sounded totally phony. "Penny's just about cleaned me out and besides we've got a big day ahead."

Mr. Shaw look at him inquisitively, but Gerry just smiled and began to put the game away.

They waited until they were sure Mr. Shaw was in his room with the light out and Mrs. Jarvis was still glued to her television set in her room before they slipped down the stairs and out the door.

It was after eleven by the time they reached Jason's house and began tossing gravel at his third-storey window. A moment later his face appeared above them, then his leg came out of the open window and reached for the branch of a tree. In seconds he was on the ground.

"Okay, let's get this show on the road," he grumbled. "I thought you guys were never going to get here. The moon was up a little while ago and it was nice and bright. Now look at it. Pitch dark."

"All the better to sleuth by," Penny giggled.

"Yeah," David agreed, "I understand ghosts like the dark."

Jason muttered something under his breath, then in a louder voice asked, "Did you remember to bring flashlights?"

"Sure," David answered. "I could only find one big one, but I got a couple of pen lights that will do."

"Good. We don't want to show too much light anyway. The penlights should be real handy."

They circled around to the front of the house and started up the street toward the hill where the abandoned theatre stood.

CHAPTER FIVE

THE old theatre looked even more desolate in the black of night. As the children climbed up the hill toward it, the air around them seemed to get colder although the temperature had dropped only a few degrees from the noon high of twenty-three.

When they came within a few yards of the building Gerry asked, "Are we going in the front door or in the back way through the emergency exit?"

"Better go in the back way," David answered. "He's probably fast asleep somewhere in the theatre, but I don't think we should take any chances of him waking and hearing us."

"Yeah," Jason agreed, "he's probably holed up in one of the rooms that go off on either side of the second balcony."

"How do you know so much about the place, Jase?" Gerry wondered.

"I asked my Grandpa about it last night. He was an usher there when it was in its heyday. Of course, he was just a kid in high school, but he remembers it very well. He and the other ushers used to explore the place when they weren't busy."

The other three were looking at him inquisitively. He blushed. "Yeah, I know. Why the sudden interest? Well, I was kind of embarrassed about the way I acted yesterday. You know, like I was scared of the place. So I decided that if I knew more about it I wouldn't be bothered by it. Besides," he grinned, "I figured since we were coming back here, any information I could get might turn out to be useful."

"Great," David said. "You can be the official tour guide. Lead the way."

Jason started up the broken concrete walkway then circled the building. When he reached the emergency exit, the door was open a crack, just as David had predicted.

"Not a sound," Jason cautioned. "Get down on your hands and knees and we'll crawl back up the aisle to the foyer."

They did as they were told and soon reached the front of the theatre.

"There's not much point in looking around down here," David reasoned. "The tramp probably hangs out upstairs."

"We're not going to try to find him, are we?" Gerry asked with a slight tremor in his voice. "I thought we were just after clues. Besides, you told your Dad we wouldn't go past the main floor."

"Yeah, but we hadn't seen the 'ghost' then. Things are different now."

"And don't worry about running into him," Jason assured him. "If he's still here he'll be well hidden. We'll just check the balcony where we spotted him yesterday." He turned and started to walk toward a flight of stairs at the far left of the foyer.

They began ascending the rickety flight of stairs single file, Jason in the lead.

When he was about half way up Jason suddenly lost his balance and started to tumble backwards. David who was directly behind caught him and Gerry jumped up to help.

"Wow!" Jason shuddered. "That was close."

"What happened?" Penny asked coming up to join them.

"Broken stair," Jason replied. "It's almost completely missing." He grinned self-consciously and resumed climbing. When they reached the first balcony they split up and began to move silently down the rows between the seats, their flashlights partially shaded by their hands.

"Nothing here," David announced when they met again at the back of the balcony. "Let's try farther up."

"Gee, do you think it's safe?" Gerry asked. "I don't mean the ghost," he assured them hastily," but there could be more broken stairs, even floorboards missing."

"If we're careful we should be okay. Remember, the guy we saw was on that balcony and he wasn't falling through."

"The stairs are over here," Jason called over. "They look a little rickety, but I can't see any missing steps."

The other three walked over to where he was gesturing with his flashlight. "Be careful," David cautioned them, "and try not to make any noise. If the guy is really living here he's probably holed up near where we saw him."

"Yeah," Jason agreed. "The second balcony is where all the little rooms are. I think my Gramps said there were three on each side."

They climbed up the stairs without further incident and again split up and began their search. Penny checked the row farthest from the railing, since her fear of heights made it impossible for her to be where she could look over into the floor of the theatre fifty feet below. She had just turned to move past the first seat when she spied something on the floor beside her. She bent to pick it up, and after shining her penlight on it, she hurried down to where David was searching several rows below.

"Look," she whispered. "It's a wrapper from a package of ham, and its got the Ideal Deli label on it."

Jason and Gerry had seen Penny rush down and start talking to David and immediately joined them.

"What is it?" Jason asked.

Penny handed him the wrapper and he and Gerry examined it.

"It could have been dropped by anyone at any time," Gerry announced rather hopefully.

"Nope. It's fresh," David pointed out. "You can still smell the meat." He took the package back and shone his stronger light on it. "And, see, it's got a date on it: August 3rd. That was yesterday."

"So you were right, Dave. The guy that robbed Mr. Garibaldi really was here. Maybe he still is. Now what do we do?" Jason wanted to know.

"We're getting out of here, pronto!" Gerry answered. "If he finds us here we could really be in danger. We'd better tell Sergeant Collins what we found and let the police handle it."

"Oh, sure. Great idea," David muttered. "And how do we explain to everyone what we were doing here in the middle of the night when we're all supposed to be home in our beds?"

"Yeah, you've got a point there," Gerry agreed. "But we've gotta tell somebody. We can't go looking for the guy ourselves."

"Why not?" Jason asked. "After all, there are four of us and only one of him. Besides, we've got the advantage of surprise. If he's still around he's probably asleep in one of the rooms. We can creep up on him and jump him."

"Good idea," Penny enthused. "But maybe we should split up. Two of us take this side and two the other."

"Sure, and we're right back to where we started," Gerry noted. "How do we explain what we were doing here in the middle of the night?"

"Maybe we could come back tomorrow morning," David suggested. "We could pretend we just found the evidence."

"No good," Penny argued. "The guy could be gone by tomorrow and then they'd never catch him."

"That's true," Jason agreed. "Besides, I'm pretty sure that if we actually catch the thief everybody will be so grateful they won't give us a bad time about sneaking out and coming up here. At least I hope they won't."

"Okay," David instructed, "Penny, you and Ger take the rooms on the right, Jase and I will check out the rooms on the other side. If you find the guy, don't try to do anything on your own. Get back here as quietly as you can. Jase and I will do the same, and we'll meet back here in five minutes."

A moment later Jason and David were wending their way between the seats to the other side of the balcony, while Penny and Gerry crept over to the aisle on their right.

"Look, Ger. Those must be the rooms Jason was talking about." Penny pointed to an alcove almost invisible in the dark theatre. "Let's sneak over and see if we can hear anyone moving around behind one of the doors."

"Or snoring, I hope," Gerry added.

With Penny leading the way they crept over to the alcove, using their penlights sparingly. There were three doors lined up in front of them. Two were closed, but the nearest one was partly open.

They doused their lights and slipped over to the open door. Penny peered around the corner and tried to see inside. With the lights out her eyes gradually adjusted to the darkness and she was soon able to make out the contents of the room. It was obviously a storage place. Boxes and cartons were stacked haphazardly over most of the floor. She turned her penlight back on and motioned for Gerry to come in.

"Somebody's been here very recently," she said, after peering around. "There's about a foot of dust on everything, and you can see where it's been disturbed on that box over there."

She put down her penlight and began to force open the flaps on the old cardboard container. Gerry had moved to the rear of the room and was prodding a pile of old props.

"Hey, look, Penny," he whispered, "there's a whole bunch of ancient junk over here." He picked up a long sword, pulled it out of its sheath and waved it in the air.

"Gerry, be quiet!" Penny cautioned. "Come over here, I want to see what's in this box."

She motioned for Gerry to shine his light on the box. Then she lifted the flaps and looked in.

"Just a bunch of old clothes." She reached in and pulled out a voluminous garment. "Look, it's an old-fashioned dress. I bet this is where the tramp got that funny suit he was wearing yesterday." She shook out the dress, sending dust into the air. Gerry sneezed three times, very loudly.

Terrified, the two children stood stock still, not daring to move. After what seemed an hour but was in reality only a couple of minutes, Penny shuddered and spoke.

"If the guy that dropped that wrapper is still around he couldn't have helped hearing that."

"Yeah, you're right. We might as well go back and wait for David and Jason. No point hanging around here now."

Penny nodded and began folding up the dress to put it back in the box.

"Okay, let's go," she said and turned toward the open door.

"Oh, no!" she gasped, then screamed.

A tall figure stood blocking the doorway, and as Gerry whirled around to see what Penny was yelling about, a flashlight suddenly beamed into their eyes temporarily blinding them.

Chapter Six

THE form in the doorway moved the light away from the children and shone it up into its face. Penny gripped Gerry's arm and began to shake. His arm was ice cold.

The apparition before them was not of this world. The face was chalk white with huge black holes where the eyes should have been. As their eyes recovered from the intense beam of the flashlight they could see that the thing was wearing the same black suit they had seen on the ghost the previous day. It stood stock still, then grinned. The teeth were blood red.

Penny screamed again and the apparition moved backward into the hall. Gerry recovered enough to grab Penny's arm and cry, "Come on, we've got to get out of here!"

Penny held back for a moment then ran with Gerry out of the room, fully expecting to feel the fingers of the hideous figure clutching at her as she passed. It continued to stand grinning at them as they shot over to the stairs and half running, half falling tore down to the next balcony. They rounded the corner and with only a quick glance back ran to the stairs that would take them to the main floor.

"Watch for the broken step, Penny," Gerry warned in a breathless voice, "but for Pete's sake hurry."

"It's okay, Ger," Penny answered. "The thing is still up there. It's not following us."

Nevertheless she lost no time leaping down the last few steps and following Gerry out into the foyer where he was struggling with the front door. A moment later Jason and Gerry bounded through the door on the left.

"Holy Nellie!" Jason exclaimed panting up to them. "What was that screaming all about?"

"Oh, you guys!" Penny gasped. "It was awful; right out of Friday the Thirteenth."

"What was?" David demanded.

"The THING," Gerry answered, pulling at the door which seemed to be stuck. "It was in the doorway. It had a head like a skull; empty eye-sockets and bloody teeth." The door finally gave way. "Come on, we've got to get out of here. Right now!"

He bolted out into the night with Penny close behind. The other two had no choice but to follow.

When they were well away from the theatre David made them stop and explain everything that had happened from the time they had split up.

Between them Penny and Gerry gave them a rundown of their experience in finding the open room, the box with the clothing, Gerry sneezing and the apparition appearing in the doorway.

"Okay, now that we're out of the theatre and out of danger, let's calm down and think this through," David said, sitting down on a bench at the far side of the fair grounds. "You don't really believe you saw anything unearthly, do you? I mean, you really don't think it was a ghost."

Penny and Gerry were silent for a moment, then Penny spoke. "I don't believe in ghosts, David, but what we saw wasn't anything you'd be likely to meet up with in the mall. I've never been so scared in my life; even when I was in the Death Drop."

"Out here where it's safe, it's easy not to believe in ghosts," Gerry added, "but let me tell you, when that thing appeared in the doorway it nearly made a believer of me."

"You can say that again," Penny agreed. "It was totally gruesome."

"But it was a human being," David insisted. "Somebody trying to scare the living daylights out of you."

"Someone who wanted to keep us away from the theatre," Jason nodded.

"Someone who didn't want to be caught," Penny added.

"The ham burglar!" Gerry giggled triumphantly.

"Oh, Gerry!" the others groaned in unison.

"So let's go back and get him," Jason said, his previous fears of the place apparently forgotten.

"Naw," David answered. "We wouldn't have a chance now that he's awake and alert. The only way we would have captured him is if we could have crept up on him when he was asleep."

"Then we're gonna have to tell somebody about him after all," Gerry said. "I suppose it'll have to be your Dad, Dave. Do you think it will get us into trouble?"

"Trouble is a mild word for what he's going to say when he finds out we've been messing around that old theatre in the middle of the night. But, you're right. This is more than we can handle. We have to tell him. Not tonight, though. We'll spring the news tomorrow morning after he's had his coffee."

"What if the tramp gets away?" Penny wondered.

"We'll just have to take the chance that he won't," David answered. "It's a pretty good bet he thinks he's scared us so badly we'll never come back, and that no one would ever believe a bunch of kids' crazy story about a white faced ghost." He got up and stretched. "I don't know about you, but I'm beat. Let's go home and try to get a good night's sleep. We're gonna need it to face tomorrow."

It was after ten when David and Gerry finally struggled out of bed and downstairs. Penny, Mrs. Jarvis informed them, was still asleep, and she hoped they weren't expecting a big breakfast to be made for them this late in the day.

"It's downright unhealthy to be sleepin' in till all hours of the day," she told them as she opened the refrigerator to take out bacon and eggs, bread and butter, orange juice and milk. "And you've missed your father, David."

"Missed Dad? Why? Where did he go?"

"Got a call early this mornin'. Had to fly to Vancouver. Didn't even have time for a bite to eat." She shook her head in disgust as she began breaking eggs into a bowl.

"When will he be back? Did he say?"

"Probably two or three days. He wasn't sure."

David and Gerry exchanged looks, the unspoken question of what to do about the Roxy tramp in both their thoughts. Penny arrived at that moment and David relayed the news about his father.

"Then what are we going to do?" she asked without thinking.

"Do about what?" Mrs. Jarvis wanted to know.

"About going to the lake," David improvised quickly, giving Penny a kick under the table, then quickly changed the subject as Mrs. Jarvis plunked their juice in front of them.

"We have no choice; we have to go to the police," David said when they had picked up Jason at his house and were walking toward the downtown area.

"I suppose so," Gerry nodded, "but we're going to have a lot of weird explaining to do."

"Don't worry," Jason assured them, "I know Sergeant Collins real well and I know she'll take me seriously. After that business at the carnival last year she thinks I'm pretty great."

"Okay," David laughed. "In that case you can be the official spokesperson."

They arrived at the small building housing Pinterville's finest and climbed the steps. When they entered the foyer they saw a police officer sitting behind a desk typing. No one else was around.

"Hi, Officer Doolittle," Jason greeted the man.

"Oh, hi, Jason. Nice to see you." The policeman

got up from his chair and came over to shake Jason's hand. Jason grew about two inches and beamed at him.

"Is Sergeant Collins in?" Jason asked after he had made sure the others had noticed the warm greeting he had received.

"She's in her office with Colonel Blunt, Jason. They should be finished in a few minutes. Anything I can do?"

"Well, sure, I suppose so," Jason answered. "We found out something we think you should know."

At that moment Sergeant Collins came out of her office with Colonel Blunt. They were still engaged in a deep conversation and didn't notice the children standing in the foyer until they were nearly upon them.

"Oh, Jason Ogilvie. And David Shaw. What are you boys doing here? And who are your friends?"

Jason quickly introduced Penny and Gerry then continued eagerly, "We have something real important to tell you. It's about the guy who ripped off Mr. Garibaldi. We found out where he's hiding."

"He's holed up in the old Roxy Theatre," David blurted out.

Penny and Gerry had been hanging behind the two since they didn't know Sergeant Collins. But when David broke the news they both moved forward and nodded their heads in agreement.

"Penny and I saw him with our own eyes," Gerry told her. "He had a white face and black sockets where his eyes should have been, and he was wearing an old-fashioned suit like Fred Astaire. We thought at first it was that ghost everybody talks about, but of course we soon realized how stupid that was."

David caught Jason's eye and winked.

"We know it was the thief," Penny spoke up. "I found a wrapper from a package of ham with the Ideal Deli's name on it."

Sergeant Collins smiled at them then shook her head. "I'm sorry to disappoint you, kids, but we've already caught the thief. Officer Doolittle picked him up last evening. He was parked on the steps of the city hall, happily eating a bag of cookies from the Ideal Deli."

"Yeah, that's what we heard, but we think the real thief is still hiding up there," David said.

"Oh, I'm pretty sure we've got the right one," Sergeant Collins assured him.

"Did he confess?" Penny asked.

"Oh, no. He denied it, of course. They always do. He said he found the cookies over at the fair grounds. His story is that someone camping there left them. That doesn't wash, however. The campground was deserted by Monday and the date on the bag of cookies was August 3rd, which was Monday."

"Then who was it we saw?" Jason murmured.

"And what about the meat wrapper I found?" Penny asked.

"Oh, he may have taken shelter in the theatre, dear, but you can be certain he wasn't there last night. As to who you saw, are you really sure you saw anyone? That place is very dark and pretty spooky. It was very likely just your imagination."

The four friends looked dejected. "Well, we're sorry

to have bothered you," Jason muttered and turned to leave. The others moved to follow him, but just as they reached the door Penny turned back. Colonel Blunt and Sergeant Collins were grinning at each other and Officer Doolittle was trying hard not to break out into laughter.

Chapter Seven

"I WAS afraid no one would believe us," Gerry moaned when they were sitting in the Bluebird Café across from the police station drinking sodas. "It sounds so darned far-fetched."

"At least she didn't ask us what we were doing in the Roxy in the middle of the night," Jason sighed.

"I don't think she believed we were even there," Penny said. "They were all laughing when we left, like it was just a big joke."

"Well, we know it wasn't a joke," David said. "There is definitely someone up there in the theatre and it's no ghost."

"Hey, wait a minute," Jason cried. "I just thought of something. Sergeant Collins said the guy they caught couldn't have found the cookies at the fair grounds because it was deserted by Monday. But is wasn't! Those kids in the camper were still there until Monday evening. They could easily have dropped them and he found them just like he said. Remember, Mr. Garibaldi told us they'd bought a bunch of stuff from him that evening."

"Good thinking, Jase," David grinned. "So the guy Penny and Gerry saw tonight could still be the real thief."

"We'd better get back to the police station and tell Sergeant Collins," Jason said.

David and Penny shook their heads. "It's no use, Jase," David told him. "She'd never believe us. And I wouldn't blame her. We must have sounded really out of it, talking about a man with a white face and black holes for eyes, dressed like some dead movie star." He gave Gerry a dirty look.

Gerry blushed and stammered, "I'm sorry, but I was just trying to make an impression so they would believe us."

"You made an impression all right," Penny laughed. "So what are we going to do now?"

"We don't have much choice, do we?" David answered.

"I hope you don't mean what I think you mean," Gerry muttered.

"Don't be a wimp, Ger," Jason said, quite forgetting that he had been the one frightened of the old theatre at first. "We all know there's no ghost; just some petty thief trying to scare us away from his hiding place."

"I'm not being a wimp, but don't you think we're taking a big chance going back there? Sure, he's trying to scare us, but when he realizes it didn't work, he could become dangerous."

"It won't be dangerous if we do what we planned last night," David assured him. "Catch him when he's sleeping. It would have worked then if Gerry hadn't had a sneezing fit and woke him up."

"I think David's right," Penny agreed. "The guy has to sleep sometime, and we can be pretty sure it's not during the day when people are more likely to be snooping around."

"So we do a repeat of last night, then," Jason said.

"Got a better idea?" David asked.

Jason was waiting for them in front of his house when David and the other two came down the street. It was a little after twelve, later than they had intended.

"Gee, you guys," Jason complained as he walked to meet them, "what kept you this time?"

"Mrs. Jarvis," David answered. "I guess she thought since Dad wasn't home, she should keep a closer eye on us."

"Yeah," Penny took up the tale, "we thought she'd never go to bed. We pretended to be real sleepy about ten o'clock and went to bed, but when we tried to sneak out we found her door wide open and her sitting up watching TV."

"She must have ears like a bloodhound," Gerry remarked. "As soon as Dave reached the landing she was up and out into the hall to see what was going on."

"I told her we were just getting something to eat, and she insisted on making us cocoa and cinnamon toast."

"Anyway, we're here now," Penny said. "So let's get on with it."

Ten minutes later they were circling the theatre to the emergency exit they had used the night before.

"Okay, this time we stick together," David ordered as they crept down the aisle to the back of the theatre. "The guy, if he's still here, is probably in one of the rooms on the right. Jase and I checked all the rooms on the left last night and there was no sign of anyone having used them."

"Yeah, there were two offices and a place where someone had dumped about a million old reels of film. You could tell the rooms hadn't been disturbed for years."

They climbed noiselessly up the first flight of stairs, carefully avoiding the broken step, then stopped to listen. There wasn't a sound.

"Okay, this is where it gets tricky," Jason said. "Let's go up one at a time so as to be as silent as possible. Dave, you go first. When you get to the top hide behind one of the seats and wait for the rest of us."

"Good plan," David agreed, dousing his flashlight. "When we're all together we'll check out each of the closed doors. But don't anybody talk. We just can't take a chance on him hearing us." He turned and started up the second flight of stairs.

"Okay, Penny, you go next," Jason told her. "Then Gerry. I'll go last."

A few moments later they were all crouched together in the aisle just outside the alcove where the three rooms were located.

"We know he isn't in the first one. That's where we found all those boxes," Penny said.

"Both the other doors are closed just like last night," Gerry whispered. "Which one shall we try?"

"Doesn't matter, I guess," David answered. "Probably the middle one. He'd be more likely to have heard Gerry sneezing if he was closer."

"I'll go first," Jason offered. "You guys stay here. If I find anything I'll flash my light on and off real quick."

Before anyone could protest he was down on his hands and knees and crawling toward the alcove.

The other three sat down on the floor and prepared to wait. No one spoke as they watched for Jason's signal. In the silence the old theatre groaned and muttered like an old man in a troubled sleep. They could hear a skittering of tiny feet coming closer, then Penny gasped as something small and furry brushed against her leg.

"Shh!" David cautioned as they held their breath, waiting for some sign that Penny had been heard. A moment later they saw the quick flash of light coming from the alcove.

When they had crawled over to Jason they saw that the door of the middle room was partly open. Jason was kneeling in front of it peering through the crack where the door was hinged to the wall.

"It looks like someone is lying on the floor on a blanket or something," Jason reported and moved away so David could take his place.

"I can't see his face," David said. "He's totally covered up, but you can see he's there all right. There's a big lump under the blanket."

He backed away and motioned for the others to follow him. They crept silently back to the seating area and along the aisle on the other side of the balcony.

"There, now we can talk," David said. "Now, here's the plan. Jase and I will go back downstairs and find something to tie the guy up with. There's probably lots of ropes behind the stage. Gerry and Penny, you take this big flashlight and guard the door where he's sleeping. If he makes any move to get up hit him on the head."

"You've got to be kidding!" Gerry exclaimed.

"Don't worry," Penny assured him, taking the flashlight from David. "I don't mind belting the guy. I won't hurt him, just stun him a little."

"That's the idea, Penny," David said, admiration in his voice. "But I don't think you'll have any trouble. He seems to be dead to the world."

The two boys got up and went down the duplicate flight of stairs on the left side of the theatre. Penny and Gerry crept along between the seats until they reached the other side.

"Okay, Ger, you watch through the crack and I'll stand outside the door. If you see him moving creep over and signal me. We'll rush in before he has a chance to get up. You jump on him and I'll hit him on the head." Gerry nodded, moved toward the room in the alcove and knelt on the left side of the door. Penny took her position a few feet away on the other side of the door.

"He hasn't moved," Gerry whispered peering through the crack. "David was right; he's sleeping like a log."

"Not quite," a voice behind him whispered and Gerry felt a hand grab him by the shoulder and a cloth was thrust into his mouth.

Chapter Eight

"GERRY?" Penny whispered, a tremor in her voice. "Is anything wrong?"

The door beside her was thrown open and she was shoved from behind. A moment later she felt a body bang into her nearly knocking her onto the floor. Before she could utter a sound the door slammed shut. A light appeared on a table beside her and she saw Gerry on his hands and knees at her feet.

Standing over him was the man in the dusty black suit.

Slowly Gerry rose and pulling the rag from his mouth gazed up at the indistinct figure.

"You just had to come back, didn't you?" It was more a statement than a question. "Why couldn't you have been frightened and stayed away?"

"Wh-what do you mean?" Penny managed to choke out.

"You seemed so scared when you were here last night. I was sure you'd never return. Now, here you are. And what am I going to do with you?"

"You could let us go," Gerry suggested hopefully, his shaking voice betraying his fear.

"I'm afraid I couldn't do that. You'd have the police here in five minutes." He sounded almost apologetic.

"You're the one who took the stuff from the Ideal Deli, aren't you?" Penny asked. The figure before them seemed less terrifying as he continued to speak in a soft, sad voice.

"Yes, I'm sorry to say. I'm not a thief, but I had to get something to eat. It was the only way." He paused for a moment as though pondering his options. He walked over to the table to light another candle, and the children were able to get a good look at him. He was tall and slight with a mop of brown hair and a three-day growth of beard. He was wearing the same clothes as the 'ghost' they had seen on the other two occasions. But rather than looking dangerous he looked pitiful and sad.

"I guess there's only one thing to do," he continued. "I'll have to put you where you can't get away."

Penny gasped and he hastened to reassure her. "Please don't be afraid. You won't come to any harm. I'll call the police in the morning so you'll be sure to be rescued. But I have to have time to find another place to go."

"You'll never get away with it," Gerry announced boldly. "Our friends will . . ."

Penny kicked him sharply in the ankle.

"What friends?" The man looked anxiously at Gerry.

"Our friends where we're staying," Penny answered quickly. "They'll find out we're not in bed when they check on us and they'll alert the police and then . . ." She stopped and took a breath. Would he believe her?

Had she covered up for Gerry's blunder in almost telling the man about Jason and David?

"Maybe so, but I'll still have time to get away before they discover where you are. Look, I'm really sorry to have to do this, but I have no choice."

He went over to the right side of the room and kicked a worn looking rug out of the way. Then he reached down and pulled on a rusty handle opening up a trap door.

"You'll be perfectly safe. And it's only for a few hours. Please forgive me, but I can't have you giving me away."

"Wh-where are you taking us?" Penny choked out.

"Down where you will be safe, but not easily discovered. Now please don't give me any trouble." He turned to Gerry. "You first."

Gerry moved slowly over to the opening in the floor. A flight of steps led down into the darkness. He hesitated for a moment, then spurred on by a slight push from their captor he started down the stairs.

"All right, miss, you're next." Penny clutched the silver barrette she had pulled from her hair, and as she walked over to the trap door she dropped it on the floor.

Jason reached the second balcony and turned to David who was following him, carrying a large coil of rope and a roll of very old adhesive tape. "Shh, be quiet," he cautioned. "He must still be asleep or else we would have heard Penny and Gerry."

David joined him and they moved together toward

the small alcove.

"There's no one here," David whispered.

"But look, there's a light coming through the door," Jason said. He peeked cautiously into the room. The form was still under the blanket but there was no sign of Gerry and Penny. He hesitated for just a second then pushed the door open. The form didn't move. Gripping his flashlight like a weapon he crept quietly over to the still figure and pulled away the blanket, revealing a wad of old clothing bunched up together to look like a body.

"Dave, come here, quick."

David rushed into the room and peered over Jason's shoulder. The two boys stared at each other in the dim light of the candles.

"It was a trap," Jason exclaimed. "The guy must have been waiting for us."

"And Penny and Gerry fell right into it. But where could he have taken them? If he'd brought them downstairs we would have seen or heard them."

"Maybe they're in one of the other rooms."

"I guess so. He must have caught them guarding the doorway and dragged them off. Let's go check."

Jason nodded and was turning to leave the room when his eye caught something shining on the floor. He bent down to pick it up and shone his flashlight on it.

"Dave, look. It's a girl's barrette."

"Let's see." David reached out and took the hair ornament. "It's Penny's," he said. "She must have come into the room."

"Or been forced in here. But why would our thief bring them in here and then take them out again?"

David shook his head in bewilderment. “Unless,” he mused after a moment, “they didn’t leave the room.”

“Sure, Dave. They all of a sudden became invisible. Our ghost is really a magician. That’s why he wears that weird suit.”

David ignored him and began searching for a hidden door. He tapped the walls and felt for hidden buttons in the best tradition of all the detective stories he’d read.

“There must be a way out of here, Jase,” he muttered. “Help me look.”

“Okay, but I think we’re wasting our time. We should be getting out of here and heading for the nearest phone.”

David stopped his frantic search. “You’re right, of course. I guess I got carried away. Penny and Gerry could be in danger while I run around playing Sherlock Holmes.”

He turned swiftly around from the wall he had been examining. As he started for the door his foot caught on a tattered square of carpeting. He tried to catch his balance, but ended up flat on his face on the floor. And there, two inches from his nose, was the rusty iron handle.

“Jason, look!” He jumped up and bending over pulled on the handle. A trap door opened in front of him. In the dim light he could see the beginning of a flight of steps leading down into a dark hole.

“This is how he must have got them out of here,” Jason breathed as he stared into the black pit below. “It must go down to some sort of basement, but I don’t remember my Gramps saying anything about such a room.”

“Maybe he didn’t know about it. It doesn’t matter. Gerry and Penny are down there somewhere and I think we should go look for them. If we wait to call the police anything could happen to them.”

“Okay,” Jason agreed with a sigh, “but for Pete’s sake be quiet. We won’t be much help to Penny and Gerry if we get caught ourselves.”

Slowly and carefully the two boys began descending the shaky stairway into the dark unknown.

CHAPTER NINE

WITH only the faint beams of their flashlights to guide them Penny and Gerry crept gingerly down the worn stairs, their captor bringing up the rear. The stairs seemed to go on forever. At the first turn Penny's foot hit a fault in a step and she grabbed for the banister. The ancient wood cracked under her weight and she felt herself falling sideways.

She started to scream. Instantly, a strong arm shot out and caught her, pulling her back onto her feet.

"Careful, miss, those old railings are as flimsy as a spider web. Best you walk over on the right side of the stairs. It's safer."

Penny turned and automatically smiled her thanks. Her captor smiled sadly back. They continued descending until they came to another turn. Penny figured they must be at ground level and expected the man to lead them into the main section of the theatre. Instead, he urged them down a third flight of stairs.

"Where are we?" she demanded, as they reached the bottom of the stairs. A strong musty smell reminiscent of old clothes and mice hit them.

"We're in the basement of the theatre," the man

answered. "I'll lead the way from here. You two follow close behind, and please don't try anything. The last thing I want to do is hurt you." He moved in front of Gerry and began to weave his way through a narrow path between an astonishing array of theatrical props. There were suits of armour, benches and chairs, desks and wardrobes, painted sets, a wooden horse, a well complete with bucket, a wheelchair dating back to the previous century, a dozen old trunks and what seemed to be about a thousand cardboard boxes of every size and shape imaginable.

"What is this stuff?" Gerry gasped as his flashlight illuminated one oddity after another.

"Old stage props," the man answered. "This place used to be a real theatre, putting on live productions, before it was turned into a movie house."

They had come to a wall at the far end of the room. The man stopped and shone his light back and forth. "Ah, here we are," he said as the light shone on a small door over to the left. He produced a key from the pocket of his jacket and unlocked it. "All right, in you go," he commanded as the door creaked open. "You'll find it quite comfortable, I assure you."

Penny went in first and shone her light around. There was a mattress on the floor and a table and chair opposite. A wooden box standing in the corner contained a few items of food; crackers, cheese, cartons of yogurt, peanut butter, bread, plus a supply of candles and a box a matches.

Gerry came up behind her and whispered, "He's gonna lock us up in here, Penny. And we only have his word that he'll tell someone where we are." He was clearly very frightened.

"It's okay, Ger. I really don't think he wants to hurt us."

"I don't," the man assured them. "And you have my solemn promise I'll alert the authorities in the morning when I'm a safe distance away." He smiled his sad smile and murmuring, "Try to sleep; it will make the time pass quickly," he closed the door. The children heard the key turn in the lock and his footsteps receding.

Wordlessly, they slumped down onto the mattress. "I sure hope you're right about the guy keeping his word." Gerry's voice betrayed his fear.

"Of course, I'm right. He'd never leave us here to die. Besides," she added hopefully," Jason and David know we're here somewhere. They'll get help and we'll be found in no time."

"Yeah? And suppose they can't find that trap door. The guy will be sure to cover it up before he leaves."

"There must be another entrance to the basement, Ger. Probably from the main floor. Don't worry. We'll be out of here in no time."

"Sure," Gerry nodded. "Unless of course he catches David and Jason."

"They came this way all right," David said as he led the way down the stairs. "You can see where the dust has been disturbed."

"Yeah, and look over here," Jason pointed out as they rounded the bend to the second flight of stairs. "The banister has been recently broken. You can tell by the colour of the wood."

"Better douse the light, Jase," David suggested when they reached the next landing. "They can't be very far ahead of us."

Reluctantly, Jason turned off his flashlight and the boys felt their way to the bottom of the flight of stairs in darkness. As he started to move forward David ran into a large object standing in front of the stairs. He reached out and his hand hit a body. He jumped back, nearly knocking Jason over in his haste to get away. Jason quickly turned on his flashlight to see what had frightened his friend. The beam revealed a dress shop dummy in an old-fashioned hoop skirt and shawl.

David gave an embarrassed laugh and muttered, "Sorry, Jase. I thought we'd run into the ham burglar."

The short flash of light had revealed the semblance of a path through the stacks of boxes, furniture and other cast offs. They started down the path feeling their way until they came to a turn. Ahead of them they saw a light go on. They were able to make out a doorway and through the door they saw first Penny then Gerry appear behind a tall figure.

"There they are," Jason whispered. "It looks like he's got them in a room. What'll we do?"

"We can't rush him," David answered. "He's too big. We'll have to catch him some other way."

"Yeah, but how? We haven't got much time. He could be planning to kill them right now. The guy's probably desperate."

"I doubt a tramp that steals food from a deli is likely to commit murder," David answered. "He's probably gonna lock them up in there then run away."

As he was speaking the door closed and the light was extinguished.

"You're right. He's coming back this way," Jason whispered. "Quick, Dave. Give me the end of that rope. I've got an idea."

David handed him the end of the coil of rope he was carrying over his shoulder. "What are we going to do?"

"Follow me, and be very, very quiet, and very, very fast."

Jason crept silently back down the path, feeling the objects on his right and left as he passed them. A few feet from the flight of stairs he found what he was looking for.

"Dave, get inside that thing and keep a tight hold on the rope."

"What are you . . .?"

"Never mind. There's no time for explanations. Just do it."

David shrugged and climbed inside the tall wardrobe trunk Jason had pointed out. Jason meanwhile was pushing his body into the tight space between the drawers of a double pedestal desk. He had barely managed to get himself in and turned around when he heard footsteps only a few feet away. He held his end of the rope near the ground and pulled it taut.

"Now, if only Dave doesn't let go, this might work," he whispered to himself.

The footsteps came closer. Jason held his breath. The rope stayed taut. There was a sudden crash, then a yell, then nothing. Jason crept carefully out of his hiding place and turned his flashlight on the form lying at his feet. A second later David joined him.

"Nice going, Jase," David grinned as they slapped each others palms.

The figure on the floor was lying face down and not moving. A small trickle of blood was falling onto the floor.

"We'd better get some help," David said. "He might be badly hurt."

"Let's get Penny and Gerry first. They must be going nuts in there, wondering if they'll ever be found."

"The door is probably locked. We'd better see if we can find a key." David reached into the jacket pocket of the prone figure. "Success!" he exclaimed producing a large old-fashioned skeleton key. He tossed it to Jason. "You get the guys; I'll stay and keep an eye on our friend here."

Jason caught the key and rushed down the narrow pathway to the end of the room where he could now see light coming from under a door. He slipped the key into the lock and threw the door open.

"Jason!" Penny and Gerry yelled in unison, jumping up from the mattress on the floor.

"Boy, are we ever glad to see you," Penny added.

"Where's the tramp?" Gerry asked. "Didn't you run into him?"

"Actually, he ran into us," Jason laughed. "He's out cold on the floor. Dave's watching him. We have to get out of here and get some help. He fell and hit his head, and he might be hurt."

He took a quick look around the room before turning to go. "Gee, the guy really made himself at home, didn't he?"

"Yeah," Gerry answered, following him out the door. "He's probably been living here for ages. He had everything he needed, and he was pretty safe from getting caught."

"He was kind of sad," Penny noted as they moved in single file down the pathway. "I felt a little sorry for him."

"Sorry for him!" Gerry exclaimed. "The guy was going to leave us to die in that hole."

"Oh, I don't think so. He said he . . ."

She was interrupted by a cry from David up ahead.

"Quick, you guys, come here. You aren't going to believe this, Jase."

"What?" Jason asked as he came up to where David was kneeling beside their prisoner. He had turned the man on his back in order to check the wound on his forehead.

David shone his flashlight on the man's face.

"Holy cow! I don't believe it!" Jason cried.

"What is it?" Penny demanded. "Who is the guy?"

"It's Ronnie Albright," Jason answered.

Chapter Ten

"RONNIE Albright? But that's impossible," Penny exclaimed. "He left town after the robbery."

"Maybe so," David answered, "but he's here now."

"And he's coming to," Jason noted.

"Oh, what happened?" The young man whom the boys identified as Ronnie Albright struggled to a sitting position and looked around at the four faces staring at him. "Jason Ogilvie and David Shaw. Where did you come from?" He shook his head groggily.

"More important, where did you come from, Ronnie?" Jason asked. "The last we heard you'd left town after the lottery money disappeared."

"I — I'm not sure. My head." He reached up and felt his forehead. "I must have fallen." He struggled to stand up.

"Hold it, Ronnie," Jason ordered. "We're going to have to tie you up and call the police. Dave, you take the flashlight and if he tries anything, give him a little tap on the head."

"Oh, but don't hurt him!" Penny cried. "He's already bleeding. He could have a concussion."

"No, I'm okay now," Ronnie said. "But please, before you call anyone hear my side of the story."

The four children looked at each other. Penny nodded her head eagerly. "Oh, Jase, give him a chance!"

"Well, okay," Jason agreed reluctantly, "but we're still going to have to tie your hands."

Ronnie nodded and put his hands behind his back. "Now if we could go back upstairs I'll tell you everything."

The four children with their captive meekly leading the way returned to the small room off the alcove on the second balcony.

"Okay," David began after they had all settled down on the floor with Ronnie in the middle of the circle. "When did you get back in town?"

"I never left. I've been here the whole time. I was tempted to run away when I heard about the theft. I knew I would be the first person they would suspect and I had no alibi, but I also knew it would be hopeless to run. They'd catch me, and it would go even worse for me."

"So why hide here?" David asked.

"I needed some time to figure out what to do. I had pretty well decided to give myself up to Colonel Blunt. I knew he'd go to bat for me. After all, he was the one who warned me that the money was missing and I'd be a suspect."

"Colonel Blunt warned you?" Penny asked in a surprised voice.

"Sure, he's the only person in this town who believes in me. He said I should get away until the whole thing blew over and the real thief was caught. Look, do you think you could loosen these ropes? They're cutting into my wrists. I promise I won't try to get away."

"Yeah, so why were you going to lock us up in that room for the night if you weren't planning to escape?" Gerry wanted to know.

"I didn't want you to go to the police before I had a chance to contact Colonel Blunt," he explained.

"There's something I don't understand," Penny said, shifting from her crouched position so she was sitting on the floor in front of Ronnie. "You said Colonel Blunt warned you that the money was missing. When was that?"

"Sunday night about eleven o'clock. I'd just gone to bed. I'd had a real busy week and was exhausted. The Colonel and I had checked the safe before we closed up the Chamber office at six o'clock and the money was all there then. Someone must have come in after we'd left and broken into the safe."

"You guys, don't you see what that means?" Penny demanded.

The other three looked baffled, then David nodded. "Of course. Colonel Blunt told everyone the theft wasn't discovered until Monday morning. How could he have warned Ronnie about it Sunday night?"

"So you're lying," Gerry accused.

"No, I don't think so," Penny answered thoughtfully. "If Ronnie really stole the money why would he stay in town? Wouldn't a real thief get as far away from the crime as possible?"

"And another thing," David added, turning to Ronnie. "Colonel Blunt told my Dad that he'd had a call from you. He said you admitted taking the money and that you were phoning long distance."

"That's crazy!" Ronnie shouted. "I've been holed up

in this place ever since Sunday evening. You saw me yesterday and the day before. How could I have made any long distance calls?"

Jason reached over and began untying Ronnie's wrists. "Boy, have you been set up!" he exclaimed.

"And by your good friend, Colonel Blunt," David agreed.

"What I don't understand is why Colonel Blunt phoned you in the first place," Jason said. "Why didn't he let you come in Monday morning when they found the money missing and then make you take the blame."

"That's easy," David answered. "If the police thought Ronnie had left town, they would stop looking for anyone else. That way the Colonel, who incidentally was the only other person with the combination to the safe, wouldn't be suspected."

"And, of course, that's why he pretended Ronnie had called him long distance. To convince everyone he really had skipped town."

"And I was going to throw myself on his mercy." Ronnie laughed mirthlessly.

"The Colonel probably thinks you did leave town," Gerry mused. "And he thinks he's perfectly safe."

"So what do we do now?" Penny wondered.

"Well, one thing we don't do is tell anyone where Ronnie is." Jason turned to the young man who was looking at him fearfully. "You'll have to stay here, Ronnie. It's a good hiding place."

"But we'll have to tell the police what happened," Gerry insisted. "They can arrest Colonel Blunt and Ronnie will be free."

"I don't think it would work that way, Ger," Jason

answered. "It's just Ronnie's word against the Colonel's."

"That's right," Ronnie nodded. "And who are they likely to believe? A pillar of the community or a guy with a record?"

"Okay, then how do we prove Ronnie is innocent and the Colonel is the real thief?" Gerry persisted.

"The money," Penny answered. "We have to find the money. Colonel Blunt must have it stashed away somewhere safe. He couldn't put it in the bank, of course, and he hasn't been out of town since the money was taken."

"That's good thinking, Penny." David nodded his head. "But where?"

"That's what the Lemon Street Gang is going to find out," Jason answered confidently. "Pinterville is a small town. There can't be that many places a person can hide three hundred thousand dollars in small bills."

"We can pretty well eliminate his apartment," David said. "He lives with his mother who is the biggest snoop in Pinterville. There's no way she wouldn't have found it if he'd stashed it there."

"What about where he works?" Penny asked.

"I doubt it," David answered. "It's just a small office. Someone would be sure to spot it if he tried to hide it in a filing cabinet or a desk."

"So what do we do now?" Gerry wondered.

"Follow him!" Jason cried. "He's bound to check up on his money to make sure it's still safe. We'll watch his every move until he leads us to it."

"That could take weeks," David protested.

"I don't think so. Besides, we don't have any other way of finding it."

"I agree with Jason," Penny nodded. "I know if I had three hundred thousand dollars hidden away somewhere I'd be checking up on it every day."

"Okay, then," David said rising from his crouched position on the floor. "We'll start tomorrow early. Meanwhile, Ronnie, you'd better get back to your room in the basement. You'll be safe there."

"Or will he?" Gerry murmured. Everyone turned to look at him. "I just thought of something. Remember when we were at the police station telling that lady cop about the tramp?"

"Sure, so what?" Jason said.

"Don't you remember? Colonel Blunt was there. He must have heard everything we said. It wouldn't take a genius to figure out that the guy we saw in the Roxy could very possibly be Ronnie."

"Gee, he's right," David gasped. "He knows there was no long distance phone call. Nothing points to Ronnie actually leaving town."

"And if he thinks there's any chance of Ronnie being here," Penny finished, "he's sure gonna make certain he doesn't tell his story to the police."

"We've gotta find another place for you to hide, Ronnie," Jason announced jumping up from the floor. "Come on, you guys, we haven't got a moment to waste."

"But where?" David wanted to know.

"Well, there's our house. It's almost as old and rambling as this theatre. There are a bunch of rooms in the basement nobody ever goes into. He'd be safe there."

“Oh, I couldn’t put you in such a dangerous position,” Ronnie protested. “I’ll just stay here for the time being. No one is going to find me in that basement room. I don’t suppose anyone even knows it exists.”

“Well, maybe you’re right, but you’re still welcome to comehome with me.”

“Thanks, Jason. I really appreciate what you’re trying to do for me. All of you. I’ll stay here for another day, then if you’ve had no luck finding the money, I’ll give myself up to the police and take my chances on them believing my story.”

“I think not,” a gruff voice spoke from behind them.

They all whirled around. In the doorway stood Colonel Blunt and he was holding a gun.

CHAPTER ELEVEN

"I WOULD like to thank you children for leading me to Mr. Albright," Colonel Blunt said cheerfully. "It will save me a great deal of trouble."

"What do you mean?" Jason asked, his voice trembling.

"Isn't it obvious? Ronnie, at large, would always be a threat to me. Oh, a very minor threat, granted. But still a threat. Now, here he is, and I no longer need to worry. Now, each of you take one of those candles and follow me." He indicated for them to come out of the room into the alcove, then ushered them into the storage room next door.

"I think you'll be safer here. Put your candles on that box over there and now, you two sit down, back to back." He pointed to Penny and Gerry. "And you, take this rope and tie them up." He tossed a rope to Ronnie. "Tie them together by their wrists and around their waists and bind their ankles. See that you do a good job. I'll be checking on your work."

When Ronnie had Gerry and Penny tightly trussed up Blunt had him do the same to Jason and David. Then after making sure the knots were tight, he made

Ronnie lie on the floor and proceeded to bind him hand and foot. "And just in case you find a way to get loose, I think a little tap on the head might be wise." He picked up the flashlight Jason had dropped when he was being bound and brought it sharply down on Ronnie's head.

"You didn't have to do that!" Penny cried. "He already has a bump on the head."

"Pity," Colonel Blunt smiled nastily. "Just be glad I'm sparing you."

"What do you mean, sparing us?" Jason demanded. "You're leaving us here to die!"

"Oh, I shouldn't be so dramatic, if I were you," Colonel Blunt answered. "You'll eventually be found. But not until I've retrieved the money and am enjoying myself in South America."

"You won't have time to get away," Penny snarled. "Our families are probably searching for us this very minute."

"Oh, I'll have plenty of time. The money, you see, is right here in the theatre, and I've already purchased my plane ticket. I should be in Calgary in less than an hour and on my way to safety before you're ever discovered."

"The stolen money is here?" Jason gasped.

"Indeed it is. In the storage space under the stage. A perfect hiding place, if I do say so myself. Now, enough of this chit chat. It's getting late." He walked over to the table and blew out the candles. "Sorry to have to leave you in the dark, but we wouldn't want you trying to burn away your ropes, would we?" He laughed nastily again, and a moment later they heard the door close behind him.

"He won't get away with this," David growled. "Someone is bound to think of looking for us here. We've talked enough about coming to this place."

"Of course," Jason agreed. "When they discover we're missing the whole town will be searching for us."

"In the meantime we have to sit here trussed up like Christmas turkeys," Gerry moaned. "Nobody will show up till morning and my arms have already gone to sleep."

"Yeah," Jason agreed, "everybody thinks we're home in our beds."

"We've got to do something," Penny cried. "Ronnie could be really hurt."

"I know, but there's nothing we can do about it but wait," David said. "There's no way we can get out of these ropes."

"I'm not so sure about that," Penny muttered. "Gerry, do you think if we worked together we could manage to move across the room?"

"Maybe, but what good is that going to do? There's no way we could open the door with our hands tied the way they are."

"I know, but I have another idea. Remember yesterday when I was looking through that box of old clothes and you found that sword?"

"Oh, yeah. I'd forgotten about that."

"Do you think we could find it again?"

"It's awfully dark, Penny, but we can sure try."

"Hey, you guys," David cried, "that's great. Anything we can do?"

"No, Dave," Penny answered. "If we can just find the sword, and if it's still sharp and if we can manage to get our hands close enough to cut the ropes. . ." She stopped and sighed. "A lot of ifs but we've gotta try. Ronnie needs help."

"Okay, Penny," Gerry ordered. "On the count of three we brace out feet and try to bump ourselves to the left. The sword is over that way. Ready? One, two, three!"

Using their bound feet as levers they managed to move themselves a few inches.

"Okay, now again." Gerry counted and they moved another short distance.

"At this rate we'll be here all night," Penny groaned. "Maybe if we fell over on our sides we could make better progress."

"Okay, let's give it a try."

"There, that's a little better," Penny said when they had managed to push themselves along another foot.

"The sword should be behind that box you found with the clothes," Gerry told her. "I think it's pretty close now."

They continued to push and struggle and slide their way into the middle of the room. David and Jason were silent, urging them on with the sheer energy of their thoughts. Ronnie groaned once but didn't wake up. An eternity went by.

Then at last, Penny spoke. "I think this is the box here beside me, Gerry. Now, all we have to do is get around it and find the sword. You didn't put it away, did you?"

"No, I don't think so. I remember sneezing then

waiting forever to see if anyone heard us. Then the guy showed up at the door. I think I just dropped the sword where I was standing."

"Good. Then it shouldn't be too hard to find. Let's start moving around the box."

Their progress was a bit easier with the heavy box of clothing acting as a lever for them to push themselves by. In a couple of minutes they were around the end of the box and moving ahead.

"It should be around here somewhere," Gerry said. Unable to see in the total darkness and with only their bodies to tell them where anything was they pushed themselves back and forth in the hope of hitting the elusive weapon.

"We're not having any luck!" Gerry cried in frustration as they continued their painful search.

"We'll find it," Penny assured bravely. "We have to," she added to herself in a much less confident voice.

"It's no use," Gerry sighed after another five minutes of searching. "I must have put it up somewhere."

"It's okay, you guys. Take it easy," David called to them. "You tried. Besides, it must be getting close to morning. It feels like we've been in this theatre for hours."

"Dave's right. We'll be rescued any minute now," Jason added hopefully. "There's nothing to worry about."

"Except Ronnie," Penny reminded him. "He could be . . ."

"Dave! Do you smell what I smell?" Jason interrupted, panic making his voice tremble.

"No, what . . .? Oh, my gosh. It's smoke!"

"Smoke? Oh, no!" Gerry cried.

"Maybe it's coming from outside," Penny suggested.

"No, there are no windows in here," Jason told her. "It's coming from the hall."

"He's set the theatre on fire!" David shouted. "The dirty rotten sleezebag! We should have known he wouldn't leave us alive to tell everyone what we'd found out about him. He had to get rid of us."

"And he's doing it by setting the place on fire," Jason wailed. "Now he'll be home free."

"Gerry, we've just got to find that sword," Penny cried. "It's our only hope. Now, let's try circling around to the left."

The smell of smoke was getting stronger. "Come on, Dave, let's try to help them look," Jason said.

The two boys began the same sort of crab-like crawl that Penny and Gerry had begun with. Their added height and stronger legs made progress much faster. They were half-way across the room when Gerry let out a war whoop.

"It's here! I hit it with my head. Now all we have to do is get it in position against the ropes on our hands and hope it still cuts."

With a good deal of grunting and groaning they managed to manoeuvre their bodies so the sword was lying against the ropes on their sides.

"Good," Gerry said. "Now we have to try to push against the blade."

They managed to shift their bodies in unison but the weapon merely slid away. A second try resulted in the same thing.

Meanwhile, Jason and David had rounded the box and were moving closer. When they bumped into Gerry and Penny, Jason said, "Okay, what can we do?"

"Can you kind of sit on the handle so it won't move around?" Gerry asked.

Another precious minute passed as the boys got in position. Penny and Gerry renewed their see-saw motion against the blade.

This time the sword stayed put.

"Hurry," David urged as the smoke grew thicker.

"We're doing the best we can!" Penny muttered angrily. A moment later she let out an ecstatic cry. "It's loosening!" Another minute or so of frantic pushing and the ropes around their waists and wrists fell off. A moment later they had their ankles freed. Penny dug into her pocket and found her small flashlight. It took only seconds to cut the ropes from David and Jason, then they ran back to where Ronnie was still lying on the floor and untied him.

Chapter Twelve

"RONNIE, wake up!" David bent over the still figure and slapped his cheek. Ronnie's eyes fluttered open and he groaned.

"Come on, Ronnie," Jason urged, "we've got to get out of here."

Gerry groped around the floor and managed to locate the large flashlight David had given him. Colonel Blunt had taken Jason's, but they still had the big one and the pen lights. Gerry gave David his pen light and beamed the larger light on Ronnie. The strong beam illuminated the ashen face of the man and the ugly red bump on the side of his head. Blood had trickled down his cheek and dried in a ragged line.

"We've got to get him up somehow. If we can get him on his feet we can carry him, I think," David said.

The three boys hoisted Ronnie into a standing position while Penny ran for the door and started to open it.

"Feel for heat, Penny!" Jason shouted when he saw what she was about to do. "If the door's hot, don't open it."

Penny put her hand on the panel above the knob. "Ouch! It's hot all right. Now what do we do?"

"We can't get out that way," Jason answered, putting Ronnie's arm around his shoulder as David had done. "We'll have to go back through the trap door. There must be an exit from it to the main floor."

Penny nodded and felt her way across the room with the aid of her flickering pen light to the spot where the trap door was located. It took her a minute to find the handle, then she had the door open.

"There's no smoke coming out here," she told them. "I think it's safe."

Jason and David, with Gerry guiding the way, staggered over to the opening, Ronnie leaning drunkenly between them.

"I don't know how we're going to manage this," Jason muttered. "This guy is a dead weight."

"Maybe we should try to carry him by his hands and feet," David suggested. "Gerry and Penny could help."

"We'd never make it down those stairs carrying him, Dave," Jason said. "It's too narrow."

They lowered the inert body of the man onto the floor. David began slapping his face and calling to him.

"Please, Ronnie, wake up! Come ON!"

The other three held their breath and waited. Finally, when they were about to give up hope of his ever gaining consciousness, they saw him stir. His eyes flickered open and shifted around to take in his surroundings.

"Oh, my head!" he moaned and straightened up.

"Where are we?"

"Thank goodness you came to!" David cried. "We're still in the storage room, but we've got to get out of here as quickly as we can. Blunt has started a fire in the theatre."

Ronnie shook his head, trying to make sense of what David was saying. Then, seeming to come a little more alive he mumbled, "Fire? Here?"

"Yeah," Jason nodded. "And we can't get out the door. The fire must be in the hall by now. We have to go down the stairs here."

"Can you walk on your own?" David asked.

"I guess so, but I'm pretty weak. If I could hold on to your shoulder I think I could make it."

Penny was holding the trap door open as David and Jason helped Ronnie to his feet and onto the first stair. "Keep close to the wall, Ronnie," Jason warned him. "Remember the broken bannister."

Slowly Ronnie manoeuvered down the stairs, Jason in front and David supporting him from the side. Gerry and Penny followed behind.

"Is there an exit to the main floor?" David asked.

"Not from here," Ronnie replied. "This stairway goes directly from the storeroom to the basement. I guess it was only used for moving stuff back and forth. There's another stairway from the main floor to the basement, though. It's across on the other side of the theatre."

"He must have started the fire in the balcony," David reasoned, "so we should be fairly safe once we get downstairs. I suppose he didn't want it discovered until we were toast."

"Oh, David, did you have to say that?" Penny groaned. "We could still be in danger."

Slowly and carefully the five worked their way down the three flights of stairs. When they finally reached the basement Jason stopped and sniffed. "I don't smell anything here. Looks like we were right. The fire hasn't come down this far yet."

Ronnie was beginning to sag again and David motioned for Jason to come and give him a hand.

"There's a sort of opening to the other stairwell over there just past the suit of armour," Ronnie muttered. "You'll have to be careful; it's pretty cluttered up."

Gerry went ahead and found the small opening. The others followed close behind. As they approached the bottom of the ancient flight of steps Jason paused again. "I think I smell smoke now," he informed them. "The fire may have worked its way down to the main floor. This may not be safe."

"We have to try it," David reasoned. "There's no other way out."

Jason nodded in agreement and together they helped Ronnie up the stairs.

Gerry reached the door to the main floor first and felt the wood. "It's warm but not hot," he informed them and grabbed the knob. The door stuck for a moment then flew open. First Gerry, then the two boys with Ronnie between them, then Penny staggered into the smoke-filled lobby.

"Keep low," David ordered, "and cover your nose with something. Remember, most people who die in fires don't burn to death; they suffocate."

"Thanks for sharing that with us, Dave," Jason muttered sarcastically. But he pulled a handkerchief from his pocket and bent over.

The lobby was only a few yards across but it seemed like they were stumbling for hours before they reached the outer doors on the left side of the theatre. When they finally got there they found them locked.

"We'll have to try the ones on the right," David choked. "Stay close and hurry."

The smoke was filling the lobby but there were still no visible flames. Their eyes were watering so badly they could barely see. Just as they approached the second set of doors, Penny stumbled and fell to the ground. No one noticed until Jason heard her feeble cry.

"Gerry, quick. Go get Penny. I think she's in trouble."

Gerry dropped to this hands and knees and crawled back the way he had come. He found Penny sitting on the floor clutching her ankle.

"I think it's broken," she sobbed.

"Come on, Penny, I'll help you." He lifted her to her feet and half walked, half dragged her back down the lobby. Jason had the door open and as they approached the boys Penny stumbled again. Gerry lost his footing as she lurched against him and the two of them fell to the ground. Suddenly, they heard the sound of sirens in the distance, and much closer in the main part of the theatre a feeble cry for help.

Chapter Thirteen

GERRY staggered to his feet and half carried, half dragged Penny to the open door. As they fell through into the clean cool air Gerry gasped, "There's someone in there, Jason. We heard a cry for help."

Penny nodded in agreement as the boys helped her sit on the ground a few feet from the door where David was standing over the dazed Ronnie. "I heard it, too. Do you think it was Colonel Blunt?"

"Not very likely. He'd be long gone by now." He turned and started back to the theatre.

"Where are you going?" Gerry demanded.

"To try to get him out," Jason called over his shoulder.

"You can't, Jase. The place is filled with smoke. And look, the fire truck is almost here. Let them rescue him."

Jason ignored them and ran through the open door. A moment later the fire engine roared up and disgorged the fire chief and six volunteer firemen.

The next few minutes were pandemonium. The chief was issuing orders, the men were attaching hoses, and Gerry was screaming to anyone who would listen that Jason was in the burning building.

Finally, he caught the chief's attention. "What did you say? Someone's in the building?"

"Yes, Sir. Two people. Someone is trapped on the main floor and Jason Ogilvie has gone in to try to rescue him."

The chief nodded curtly then ran ahead and spoke to one of his men. A moment later Jason appeared in the doorway. The chief turned and said something to him. Jason nodded and pointed back into the building. The chief and his companion disappeared into the building and Jason joined his friends.

"Jase, are you okay?" David demanded anxiously.

"Yeah, I'm fine. But the guy inside isn't. I managed to get as far as the aisle going into the main part of the theatre, but I couldn't get any further. I saw him lying on the floor at the bottom of the stairs. He must have tripped on that loose board and fallen."

"Who was it?" David asked.

"I'm not sure, but I think it was Colonel Blunt."

"Colonel Blunt? But I was sure he'd be on his way to Calgary by now. He was planning to get away as soon as he retrieved the money," Penny said.

A large crowd had gathered while they were talking. The firemen were trying valiantly to fight the blaze but it seemed to be a losing battle. Acrid smoke was pouring from the front of the old theatre.

The man trapped in the theatre was being carried out the door by two firemen, his leg jutting out at a crooked angle. It was, as Jason had assumed, Colonel Blunt.

An ambulance had arrived on the scene right

behind the fire truck, and a team of paramedics took over from the firemen who went back to the hoses. The paramedics then tried to secure the Colonel to a stretcher. He was resisting violently and screaming, "The money! The money! Let me go! I have to get the money!"

The men finally got him tied down and into the ambulance. Then they came over to where Ronnie and Penny were seated on the ground with Jason, David and Gerry standing over them.

Penny and Ronnie were taken to the ambulance and whisked off with the Colonel to the community hospital. The paramedics wanted to take Jason as well, but he insisted he was perfectly all right. He hadn't been in the theatre long enough to have inhaled a damaging amount of smoke.

The three boys stood and watched the firemen fighting a losing battle for the rickety old theatre. It was becoming apparent that the place would be totally demolished. The old wood was like tinder. Five minutes went by and the front part of the roof collapsed.

"At least he didn't get the money," David sighed. "He must have started the fire in the balcony, then come downstairs to retrieve the loot and fell."

"So it must still be in the theatre and probably burned up by now," Gerry added.

"Maybe not!" Jason exclaimed. "Come on."

He turned and started to run around the back of the theatre. The other two followed.

"Look, the fire hasn't got this far yet," Jason said when they reached the emergency door. Then before the others could stop him he was through the door and leaping over to the stage a few feet away.

The vast area was filled with smoke, but the flames hadn't reached the back of the theatre yet. Jason covered his mouth and nose with his handkerchief and pulled at the small door on the underside of the stage. The open emergency door gave him just enough light to see the large suitcase sitting just inside the enclosed space. He grabbed the handle and pulled it out. A moment later he was back out the door.

"Got it!" he cried triumphantly.

When they returned to the front of the theatre they found two squad cars parked nearby and Sergeant Collins talking to the fire chief. When she spotted the boys she walked swiftly over to them. The expression on her face was not welcoming.

"You kids! What have you done?" she demanded accusingly.

"Done?" Jason's face registered surprise.

"Yes, done. I've just come from the hospital and Colonel Blunt tells me you set the theatre on fire. He claims you were trying to smuggle Ronnie Albright out and set the fire to cover your tracks. Honestly, Jason, this is just not like you. Whatever got into you to pull such a wicked stunt?"

"But Sergeant Collins," Jason protested, "it wasn't that way at all. Sure, we came here looking for the tramp we thought had stolen the stuff from the Ideal Deli, and we found Ronnie. But he explained everything to us. Colonel Blunt had set him up and taken the money himself."

"And you believed him, of course." Her tone was sarcastic. "As soon as the medics recognized Ronnie they radioed the station. I met them at the hospital and had Ronnie put under guard. Then I talked to Colonel Blunt, who incidentally is not badly hurt thanks to you kids. He told me he had seen a light in the old theatre when he was on his way home from an all-night meeting of the lottery committee and stopped in to investigate. He saw smoke seeping out from an upstairs window, then heard someone screaming for help and rushed in. When he tried to locate whoever was calling, Ronnie pushed him down the stairs from behind. I would be ready to put you all in custody if you hadn't acted in such a responsible way in saving the Colonel."

"But it's all lies!" David sputtered tearfully. "He was the one who started the fire."

"That's right," Gerry chimed in. "He tied us up and left us in a room to die." He went on to explain how they had freed themselves and escaped through the basement passage.

"That's some story," Sergeant Collins said when Gerry had finished. "But really, I find it hard to take the word of a known criminal and a bunch of thrill-seeking kids over that of one of the most respected men in the community." Then her voice softened. "I'd like to believe you. You're good kids. But you have absolutely no proof of what you're saying. I can only assume you have been misguided in your loyalty to a young man for whom you feel sorry and have made up this preposterous tale to save him."

David and Gerry started to protest, but Sergeant Collins put up her hand to stop them. "Come with me and I'll see that you're driven home. Your parents will have to be told of this escapade. I'll leave your punishment to them."

She started to turn back to the car when Jason's voice stopped her. He was kneeling on the ground opening the suitcase.

"Maybe this will convince you we're telling the truth," he said quietly as he threw the lid open, exposing a case full of loose bills.

Chapter Fourteen

"JASON, what's that?" Sergeant Collins stared in disbelief at the pile of bills.

"The money from the lottery. The money Colonel Blunt stole and tried to blame on Ronnie."

"But where did YOU get it?"

"It was hidden in the storage space under the stage in the theatre. Colonel Blunt told us where he'd hidden it when he thought we wouldn't be around to expose him."

"Yeah," David chimed in. "He just had to boast about how smart he was."

Sergeant Collins shook her head in amazement then motioned to an officer standing a few feet away. "Get this suitcase down to the station, will you, Tony. And see that Colonel Blunt is put under guard at the hospital." Then turning back to the boys she said, "Okay, let's go."

"Where are you taking us?" Jason asked, a slight tremor in his voice.

"Home, of course. Your folks must be worried sick about you."

"I don't think anyone has any idea that we aren't

safe in bed," David grinned. "My Dad's away and Mrs. Jarvis sleeps like a log."

"And my folks have no idea I'm gone," Jason added. "My room's in the attic."

Sergeant Collins tried to look stern but she couldn't stop a slight smile from crossing her lips. "You kids! You're impossible. Okay, I'll take you to the station where you can give us your statement, but then it's definitely home with you."

Between them the boys gave a complete description of every thing that had happened from the moment they entered the old theatre that evening until the police arrived at the scene.

When they were through, Sergeant Collins and the officer taking down the statements exchanged astonished looks.

"Well, he certainly had us fooled," she said at last. "No one, not even I, doubted the Colonel's word. I guess we all owe poor Ronnie Albright a very big apology."

"I'm pretty sure Ronnie will settle for just getting his job back," David suggested.

"And a good hot meal," Jason added with a grin. "The poor guy's been living on cheese and cold meat for days."

"What I still don't understand," Sergeant Collins mused, "is what made you kids believe Ronnie was innocent and the Colonel was the villain in the piece."

"Oh, I guess we didn't explain that too well," David answered. "Actually it was Penny who figured out that the Colonel couldn't have known the money was missing on Sunday night when he phoned Ronnie unless he'd taken it himself. She's really smart for a girl."

Sergeant Collins gave him a scathing look.

"I mean she's really a very smart girl," he amended hastily.

"By the way, what about Penny and Ronnie?" Gerry asked.

"They're being kept over night for observation. Penny has a sprained ankle and will be home tomorrow — or I should say today," she said, checking the clock on the wall. It was almost four-thirty. "As for Ronnie, the doctors want to keep him a little longer to make sure he doesn't have a concussion. They tell me he received quite a blow on the head. Now, it's time we took you home." She stood up and motioned to the three boys. "It's been a long night and we're all tired. We can finish up any loose ends tomorrow."

"If it's all the same to you, I'd like to go home with David and Gerry," Jason said. "I'll call Mom first thing in the morning, but I don't want to wake up the household so early."

"Well, all right. I suppose that's the wise thing to do. Obviously you haven't been missed or we would have had a call from your folks."

Ten minutes later the three boys were dropped of at David's. As they tip-toed silently down the hall they could hear Mrs. Jarvis's snores echoing through the house.

David had set his clock radio for six-thirty and it seemed the boys had barely closed their eyes before it went off. Jason called his mother immediately to tell her where he was, omitting the fact that he had been out most of the night. He'd explain the whole thing when they were face to face, but in the meantime he felt it prudent to let her think he'd merely gotten up early and gone visiting.

When they arrived downstairs a few minutes later they found Mrs. Jarvis yawning over the coffee pot.

"Oh, my, you startled me!" she exclaimed as they marched into the kitchen. "You're up awfully early. And Jason's here, too." She gave them a baffled look then went to the refrigerator. "I expect you'll be starvin' to death after sleepin' so heavy. What'll it be? Bacon and eggs or French toast and sausage?"

When they had given their order Mrs. Jarvis poured orange juice and made them sit down at the table, after inspecting their hands for any sign of grime.

"And what about the wee girl? Do you suppose she'll be down or should I go wake her?"

The three boys looked at each other, then David cleared his throat.

"Ah, Mrs. Jarvis, there's something I think I should mention to you. Penny won't be down for breakfast. She's in the hospital."

"In the hospital! Lord a mercy! What are you saying?" Mrs. Jarvis clutched her heart and sank down in a chair.

"Oh, don't get upset. She's fine. She'll be home in a little while. You see, it all started when this guy in an old-fashioned black suit . . ."